CANADA AT WAR

THE WAR of 1812
1812–1814

Douglas Baldwin
Patricia Baldwin

Weigl

Published by Weigl Educational Publishers Limited
6325 10th Street SE
Calgary, Alberta
T2H 2Z9

Website: www.weigl.com

Library and Archives Canada Cataloguing in Publication

Baldwin, Douglas, 1944-
        War of 1812 / Douglas Baldwin.

(Canada and her wars)
Includes index.
Issued also in an electronic format.
ISBN 978-1-77071-628-5 (bound).--ISBN 978-1-77071-629-2 (pbk.)

        1. Canada--History--War of 1812--Juvenile literature.
I. Title. II. Series: Baldwin, Douglas, 1944- . Canada and her wars.

FC442.B35 2010   j971.03'4   C2010-903756-1

Printed in the United States of America in North Mankato, Minnesota
1 2 3 4 5 6 7 8 9 0 15 14 13 12 11

072011
WEP040711

Project Coordinator: Heather Kissock
Design: Terry Paulhus

Photograph Credits

Alamy: pages 3, 7, 8, 10T, 12B, 15, 22B, 28B, 30B, 31B, 38TR, 40L, 41M, 41R; All Canada Photos: page 29B; Archives of Ontario: pages 16,
25; Dick Bauch: page 41L; Canada's War Museum: pages 14T, 18, 19M, 19L, 20T, 20M; City of Toronto: page 19R; Corbis: page 13B; CP
Images: pages 5, 31T; Getty Images: pages 4T, 6, 10B, 12T, 20B, 21M, 24T, 26, 29T, 32L; Paul Hermans: page 32R; iStockphoto: pages 21T,
21B; Library and Archives of Canada: pages 1, 4B, 11B, 13T, 14B, 17, 22T, 23, 24B, 27, 28T, 30T, 33T, 34, 35, 37L, 37MT, 37MB, 37BL, 42, 43;
Museum de Chateau Ramezay: page 11T; Parks Canada: page 40M; D. Gordon/E. Robinson: page 40R.

Every reasonable effort has been made to trace ownership and to obtain permission to reprint copyright material. The publishers would be
pleased to have any errors or omissions brought to their attention so that they may be corrected in subsequent printings.

We acknowledge the financial support of the Government of Canada through the Canada Book Fund for our publishing activities.

TABLE OF CONTENTS

Canada at War

S ince Confederation, Canadians have served around the world in military actions for the cause of peace and freedom. Approximately 120,000 Canadians have lost their lives in these wars, and countless more have suffered grave injuries.

Nationally and internationally, Canadians are normally portrayed as a peaceful people. However, conflict has been a part of Canada's history since Europeans landed on the shores of North America in the sixteenth century. Initially, France and Great Britain fought to gain control of the New World. At the same time, the Europeans fought with the Aboriginal Peoples.

Following Great Britain's final defeat of the French forces in 1759, Canada soon faced a new enemy. In 1775, 1812, 1837, and 1866, the United States attacked Canada. In fact, one of the major reasons for Confederation in 1867 was to create a larger union that could better defend itself from the United States.

After Confederation, Canada remained a British **colony** and was automatically involved in major conflicts, such as the South African War at the beginning of the 20th century and World War I. It was in this latter war that Canadians earned their reputation as fierce warriors. Although Canada gained true independence in the 1930s, its links to Great Britain remained strong, and Canada entered World War II in 1939 as Great Britain's leading ally.

Since then, Canada has been committed to **multilateralism** and has gone to war only within large multinational coalitions such as in the Korean War, the Gulf War, the war in the Balkans, and the 2001 invasion of Afghanistan. Canada has also played an important role in United Nations peacekeeping operations, committing more troops than many other countries. As of 2006, Canada had the second-highest peacekeeping fatality rate in the world.

Prologue to War

The War of 1812 was part of the larger **Napoleonic Wars** that began in Europe. When France attempted to prevent Europe from trading with Great Britain, the British government decided to blockade European ports from receiving supplies from abroad. This angered the United States.

USING TRADE AS A WEAPON

After the British Navy defeated the French fleet in the Battle of Trafalgar in 1805, no other nation was strong enough to challenge Great Britain's control of the seas. Since France controlled the European continent, Napoleon Bonaparte, France's leader, forbade Russia, France, and other European nations from trading with Great Britain. In response, the British Navy **blockaded** European ports, preventing ships from delivering their cargoes to the continent. This hurt American businesses even more, especially those in the north and south-eastern states.

EXPANSION

As more people began moving to the United States, settlements began to extend farther inland. The country's Aboriginal Peoples were displaced as a result of this expansion. This led to conflicts between settlers and Aboriginal Peoples. When some Aboriginal Peoples gained access to firearms, the settlers complained that the British were arming and inciting the Aboriginal Peoples to prevent the expansion of inland settlements.

When President James Madison declared war on Great Britain on June 18, 1812, the British naval blockade of Europe was provided as the official reason for the war. This was not, however, the only reason for the tension between the two countries. The War of 1812 actually stemmed from a combination of issues. Some of these were remnants from previous problems between the two countries. Others resulted from the needs of a growing country and the power of an established **empire**.

IMPRESSMENT

Besides blocking U.S. ships from European ports, the British Navy routinely stopped and searched U.S. ships for **deserters**. Sometimes, the British went beyond taking their own sailors back. They also forcibly removed U.S. sailors from their own ships and recruited them into the British Navy in an act called impressment. The United States had fought for its independence from Great Britain, so impressment brought the issue of U.S. **sovereignty** to the forefront. The U.S. government asserted that its citizens no longer had to fight on the side of Great Britain and could not be forced to do so.

WAR HAWKS

Outraged by the British blockade, the impressment of U.S. citizens, and interference in U.S. plans for expansion, a group of U.S. politicians called the War Hawks were determined to fight for the country's liberties at home and at sea. The War Hawks felt that the U.S. government was reacting too slowly to British high-handedness. They believed the U.S. had to take a stronger stand against Great Britain. Their goal was to eradicate the British presence in North America. By the fall of 1811, these politicians were openly discussing the idea of invading Upper and Lower Canada, the British colonies to their north.

Key War of 1812 Battle Sites

While the War of 1812 had international connections due to the situation in Europe, the fighting took place solely in North America. Neither Canada nor the United States were the size each is today. Therefore, much of the war took place in a very localized area along the southern parts of what was then known as Upper and Lower Canada. In fact, most of the War of 1812 was fought in and around Lake Erie.

These maps shows where the battles between the Canadas and the United States took place and which side won each battle.

→ British Troop Movements

★ British Victory

★ United States Victory

→ United States Troop Movements

Michilimackinac

Detroit

Frenchtown

N

0   250 Kilometres

Lower Canada

Upper Canada

Châteauguay

Crysler's Farm

Plattsburg

Ogdensburg

York (Toronto)

Sackets Harbor

Oswego

Moraviantown

United States

Put-in-Bay

Fort Stephenson

Queenston Heights

Fort George

Fort Niagara

Stoney Creek

Beaver Dams

Lundy's Lane

Black Rock

Fort Erie

Chippawa

The War Begins

News of the U.S. declaration of war spread quickly. British couriers had been waiting in Washington to bring the news to Great Britain and its British North America colonies. Major General Isaac Brock, the commander of the British forces in Upper Canada, received the news within a week and quickly ordered an attack on Fort Michilimackinac in Michigan. By the time the American commander there received word that war had been declared, the fort was surrounded. He surrendered on July 17 without firing a shot.

British North Americans had no say in the war. They were British, not Canadian, citizens. The colonies existed for the benefit of Great Britain, which made all the major decisions. In Upper Canada, however, Brock was worried about the population's loyalty. In Lower Canada, the English elite were loyal to the British Empire, which they relied upon for employment. French Canadians supported the cause because they feared that an American victory would lead to **assimilation**, a weakened Catholic Church, and loss of land. As a result, the local government agreed to provide funds for defence and to strengthen the **militia**.

▌ Major General Isaac Brock is one of the best known military officers in Canadian history.

▌ Fort Michilimackinac was originally a British holding. Great Britain handed the fort over to the U.S. at the end of the American Revolutionary War.

On paper, it was no contest. The United States had a population of 7.5 million and a **regular army** of about 12,000, compared to 500,000 British North Americans and 4,500 British soldiers. In addition, British North America lacked the food, the armaments, and the manufacturing resources available to the United States. Upper Canada, for example, had to import almost everything from Great Britain via Montréal, including bullets, cannonballs, anchors, and boots. These supplies could easily be cut off by capturing Montréal and Québec City. In addition, the majority of Upper Canada's population had recently come from the United States, and it was unclear if the French Canadians in Lower Canada would remain loyal. The British army faced the staggering problem of defending a border that stretched from the Atlantic Ocean to the Great Lakes.

▍ Sir George Prevost was in command of all British forces in North America during the War of 1812.

▍ Many people moved to the Canadas hoping to make a better life for themselves.

Fighting for the Canadas

The War of 1812 took place on land, on the Atlantic Ocean, and in the Gulf of Mexico. Although the United States won notable victories at sea, Great Britain had a superior navy, and the United States directed most of its energies towards capturing Upper and Lower Canada. It was here that it felt more confident of victory on the basis of numbers alone.

The Battle of New Orleans took place in Louisiana, in the Gulf of Mexico. The war had officially ended, but word had not yet reached the area.

Numbers, however, could not make up for the fact that the British forces were more prepared for war than those of the United States. Their leaders were trained in strategy and used that training to predict and deter U.S. attack. They were joined in this effort by Canadian settlers and even Aboriginals.

British Forces

When the war began, the British military presence in the Canadas was minimal. There were only about 1,600 soldiers in the Canadas, with a further 2,400 stationed in the Maritimes. Their assignment prior to the war was to maintain order in the land. When war was declared, the British government rushed to send more troops over. This was difficult, however, as most of the British forces were fighting in Europe. Instead, the first reinforcements to arrive in the Canadas were from British installations in the Caribbean. Most of these soldiers had not seen battle in years. Still, as the war continued, Great Britain was able to send more reinforcements, and Canadians began forming **regiments** and militias of their own.

The British appeared to be in much better shape when it came to the war on water. When the war began, Great Britain had 85 ships in the area, while the United States had only 17. As a result, the British were able to blockade the eastern coast of the United States, attack U.S. merchant ships, and stage several raids on U.S. holdings. The U.S. naval forces won only a few battles against the British, most of them at the beginning of the war.

The British blockade of U.S. ports started almost immediately upon declaration of war. British ships wasted no time in hampering U.S. ships coming out of places such as Chesapeake Bay, and off the coasts of Maryland and Virginia.

Upper Canada Forces

In the years leading up to the War of 1812, Upper Canada had become a refuge for United Empire Loyalists. These were U.S. settlers who had supported Great Britain during the **American Revolutionary War**. When the British lost the war, the Loyalists had either fled or were forced out of the United States. About 10,000 settled in Upper Canada.

There was much concern about the Loyalists when the War of 1812 was declared. The British were not sure if the Loyalists would support the British cause. Even if they did, it was uncertain whether the Loyalists would take up arms against their former countrymen.

Ultimately, the concerns were baseless. The Loyalists formed militia units to fight alongside the British forces. They proved to be a valuable ally, for many of them had fought in Loyalist regiments during the American Revolutionary War.

Loyalists were not the only ones to fight, however. The area also had former British soldiers who had settled in Upper Canada after leaving the military. They, too, were ready to fight for their new home.

▌ Loyalists began arriving in British North America shortly after the American Revolutionary War ended in 1783. Many settled in the Maritimes and what is now southern Ontario.

"We have had a most harassing journey of 10 days to this place when we arrived last night in a snow storm. It has been snowing all day & is now half a foot deep. … Frequently I had to go middle deep in a mud hole & unload the wagon & carry heavy trunks 50 yards waist deep in the mire & reload the wagon. Sometimes put my shoulder to the fore wheel & raise it up.

- Extract from an original letter from Thomas G. Ridout (Kingston) to his father Thomas Ridout, November 1, 1813 Thomas Ridout family fonds

Reference Code: F 43, box MU 2390 Archives of Ontario

THE MARITIME COLONIES

The Maritime colonies, which were protected by the British navy in Halifax, were not invaded and generally coexisted peacefully with their New England neighbours. For example, in the town of Eastport, Maine, across the St. Croix River from New Brunswick, the citizens agreed to keep up friendly terms with their New Brunswick neighbours in St. Andrews, who allowed unarmed American vessels to trade in New Brunswick. In one military expedition, however, troops from Halifax captured much of Maine, which they held until the peace treaty.

Lower Canada Forces

The British also had reason to question the willingness of Lower Canadians to join the fight against invasion. Lower Canada was inhabited mostly by French Canadian settlers. These people had no reason to be loyal to the British. In fact, during the American Revolutionary War, many French had been sympathetic to the U.S. cause.

However, over the years, the French Canadians had become accustomed to British rule. When war was declared, they signed up for military service without issue. Most became part of militia units that had been created specifically for the War of 1812. These units were created primarily for **garrison duty**. However, many militia soldiers did see battle during the war.

One of the most well-known Lower Canada militia units was the Canadian Voltigeurs. The unit's officers came from many of the leading families in Lower Canada. The lower ranks were made up of volunteers between the ages of 17 and 35.

Initially, the Voltigeurs were assigned to defend the eastern parts of Lower Canada. However, over time, they also assisted in the defense of Upper Canada, where they fought on numerous occasions. The Voltigeurs disbanded in 1816.

▌ The Voltigeurs were paid by the Province of Lower Canada. They were not part of the regular British forces.

▌ Only a few regiments and militia were stationed in Québec City during the war. While the city was considered to be a key stronghold for both sides, the U.S. did not mount an attack against it.

■ Aboriginal Peoples played key roles in many of the war's conflicts, including the Battle of the Thames, which took place on October 5, 1813, in what is now southern Ontario.

Aboriginal Peoples

During the War of 1812, the British were able to rely on not only the Aboriginal Peoples in the Canadas, but also on many of those in the United States as well. Members of the **Iroquois Confederacy**, such as the Mohawks, were instrumental in helping the British and Canadians. They had supported the British cause mainly because they believed the British would treat them more fairly than the U.S. would in regards to land claims.

This was the reason many Aboriginals also joined the British side in the war. They felt the U.S. was taking their land away from them without any discussion or negotiation. Their future looked bleak if they were not able to control the movement of U.S. settlers.

Aboriginals who fought alongside the British came from various groups, including the Sioux, Wyandot, Wea, Potawatomi, and Shawnee. One of the most well-known Aboriginals to fight alongside the British was a Shawnee chief called Tecumseh.

TECUMSEH

Tecumseh was the chief of the Shawnee, a group of Aboriginal Peoples who lived primarily in the U.S. states of Ohio, Kentucky, and Indiana. Over the course of the War of 1812, Tecumseh became known as a fierce fighter for the British forces. In fact, when British General Brock advanced on Detroit in August 1812, Tecumseh was instrumental in the British victory.

By 1813, the British were losing the war on the Detroit **front** and began making preparations to leave the area. This retreat would leave Tecumseh and his people vulnerable to American attack. They requested additional weapons from the British so they could continue the fight on their own. The British did not supply them with weapons, but instead, agreed to one last stand with the Aboriginals against the U.S. The battle did not go well for the British, however, and they broke and ran when the battle began. Their flight left about 500 Aboriginals to face some 3,000 Americans. During the battle, Tecumseh was fatally wounded. With Tecumseh's death, Aboriginal resistance south of the Great Lakes practically ceased.

War Heroes

The men and women who participated in the War of 1812 came from a range of backgrounds. Some were professional soldiers, while others were volunteers who joined the militia. A few were not military at all. They were just people who wanted to help their side of the border win the war. While many performed heroic acts, some names became more known than others.

LAURA INGERSOLL SECORD
(1775–1868)

"I was determined to persevere."

Laura Ingersoll was born in Massachusetts, but moved to Upper Canada with her father in 1795. The family settled near the present town of Ingersoll, Ontario. In 1797, Laura married James Secord, a young merchant in Queenston.

Secord's importance to the War of 1812 began on June 21, 1813, when she overheard American officers talking about an intended surprise attack on the British outpost at Beaver Dams. Secord decided that she had to warn Lieutenant James FitzGibbon, the company commander.

The distance to the outpost by road was about 32 kilometres, but fearing she would be spotted, Secord took a roundabout route. For part of the trip, she was accompanied by her niece, but when she became exhausted, Secord continued alone through fields and woods. That evening, Secord stumbled into a group of Aboriginal people, who took her to FitzGibbon. There, she told him what she had heard. Two days later, on June 24, British soldiers and Aboriginal warriors claimed victory at Beaver Dams after they ambushed almost 500 American troops. The official report of the attack, however, made no mention of Secord's role in the ambush.

Laura Secord was 85 before she achieved public recognition for her heroic deed. While visiting Canada in 1860, the Prince of Wales learned of Secord's 32-kilometre walk and sent her a reward of £100. Secord subsequently became celebrated as a heroine in history, poetry, and drama.

Laura Secord typified pioneer women in her courage, endurance, and resolution in the face of adversity. FitzGibbon remembered her as a person of "slender frame and delicate appearance," but underneath was a strong and persistent will. She died in 1868, at the age of 93.

ISAAC BROCK (1769–1812)

Isaac Brock was the eighth son of a wealthy family in Guernsey, an island in the English Channel. At the age of 15, Brock joined the British army and quickly gained combat experience in Europe. In 1802, he and his regiment were sent to Canada. As tensions along the American border increased, Brock was given the job of building and repairing military fortifications to improve the colony's defences. By 1807, he commanded all British forces in Upper Canada.

When war broke out in June, 1812, Brock quickly organized his forces and readied for the fight. Within two months, he had scored a victory over the United States at the Battle of Detroit. Afterwards, he returned to Upper Canada to organize a defensive line against imminent U.S. attack.

On the night of October 13, 1812, approximately 3,000 U.S. soldiers began their attempt to take the town of Queenston. They took control of the heights around the town and began firing at the small British force of 300 stationed there. Brock rallied his troops and began heading up the heights toward the American soldiers. He was fatally wounded during the charge.

ROBERT HERIOT BARCLAY (1786–1837)

Robert Barclay was born in Scotland. The son of a minister, he joined the Royal Navy as an 11-year-old and later took part in the Battle of Trafalgar in 1805. In February 1813, he travelled to Kingston, Upper Canada, and assumed charge of the British naval forces on Lake Erie.

Lake Erie was not an important holding for the British. They were more concerned with maintaining control of Lake Ontario. As a result, Barclay was given limited resources to keep Lake Erie secure.

In the meantime, the U.S. was building up its fleet in the area, readying for a fight. Barclay saw that he was going to be overpowered by the strength of the U.S. fleet. He requested supplies and reinforcements from his British commanders, but did not receive the necessary support. As a result, his fleet experienced a humiliating defeat when the fight began.

Barclay was absolved from responsibility for the defeat. The British commanders agreed that he had not been given the support needed to successfully combat the American fleet.

CHARLES-MICHEL D'IRUMBERRY DE SALABERRY (1778–1829)

Charles de Salaberry was born in Beauport, in what is now Québec. He enlisted in the military at the age of 14. Two years later, he was given a **commission** and stationed in the West Indies. Here, he distinguished himself for his bravery in the invasions of the French colonies of Guadeloupe and Martinique. Later, he served in the Netherlands during the Napoleonic Wars. Returning to Lower Canada in 1810, de Salaberry joined the Voltigeurs Canadiens militia, where his zeal and energy were responsible for recruiting some 480 volunteers and 29 officers.

De Salaberry was instrumental at keeping the U.S. forces at bay during the War of 1812. In November, 1812, de Salaberry and the Voltigeurs thwarted an attempted invasion near Lacolle. In the next two months, the **company** destroyed American positions on Lake Champlain, counter-marched throughout the south shore of Montréal District, and spied on enemy positions. Later that year, de Salaberry gained lasting fame when he turned back a superior American force at Châteauguay and thus prevented the capture of Montréal. His commander, however, denied that de Salaberry deserved credit for the victory and gave it to the other officers. Humiliated, de Salaberry retired from the militia. He later became a wealthy landowner.

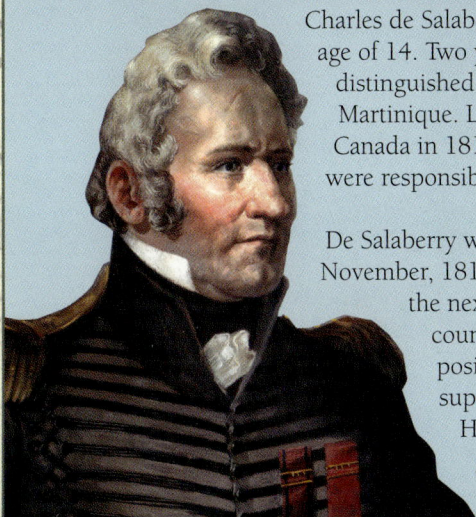

A Soldier's Uniform

People from various backgrounds fought in the war of 1812. While **civilian** fighters were mostly garbed in their everyday clothing, professional soldiers wore uniforms assigned to them by their regiment. Uniforms at this time were not made to blend a soldier into his environment. Instead, they were elaborate and colourful. The uniforms of high-ranking soldiers tended to have more embellishment than those of low-ranking men.

HEADGEAR

The standard headgear for British soldiers was called a shako. This tall hat had a stovepipe appearance and was normally made from felt. Shakos ranged in colour from white to black. A brass plate was attached to the front of each shako. The plate indicated the soldier's regiment and included a symbol denoting the British Crown. A white plume, or feather, rose from the front of the hat. Soldiers wore smaller and more compact hats as the war progressed.

WATER CANTEEN

Every soldier in the field had a canteen so that he had a supply of water with him. The canteens were made from wood, tin, or a combination of both materials. A leather carrying strap wrapped around the canteen so that it could be worn around the soldier's neck and shoulder.

COATS AND JACKETS

Jackets worn by soldiers in the War of 1812 followed the fashion of the time. They were single-breasted, with lapels. The colour of the jacket reflected the soldier's regiment association and rank. Officers in the Voltigeurs, for instance, wore green jackets. The lower ranks wore grey. Other colours included blue and red.

These jackets were not made for the cold Canadian winters. To provide additional warmth, soldiers were supplied with great coats. These heavy coats were double-breasted with regimental buttons and were normally blue or grey in colour. Many of them were lined with fur.

SHIRTS

When British soldiers first arrived in what is now Canada, they wore white, linen shirts under their uniform jackets. The material was later changed to flannel to accommodate the cold Canadian climate. The shirts came up high on the neck and had long sleeves. A frill was attached to the front of the shirt and was the only piece of the shirt to show over the jacket. The frill could extend up to 23 centimetres down the front of the uniform.

POUCHES

To hold their **cartridges**, militia regiments were issued either stiff leather pouches that were worn on the right hip attached to a shoulder belt, or boxes that were worn on the abdomen. The "belly box" was a simple wooden block drilled with holes to hold 18 rounds of ammunition.

BREECHES AND GAITERS

At the beginning of the war, soldiers wore knee-length breeches for pants. The breeches were white and made of wool. Black gaiters were worn to cover the bottom half of the leg and the top of the shoe. This stopped rocks from entering the shoe. The gaiters could be adjusted by moving a seam along the back. A strap hooked under the shoe to keep the gaiter in place. Over time, the wearability of the breeches and gaiters became a concern. Soldiers began to go against regulation and wear full-length trousers for battle. The British government took note and began supplying trousers as part of the uniform.

BOOTS AND SHOES

Soldiers were equipped with either shoes or boots for footwear. Both were made of black leather. Knee-length boots were assigned to soldiers riding horses. Ground soldiers wore ankle shoes with gaiters attached for protection.

War of 1812 Weapons

Muskets and cannons were the most used weapons in the War of 1812. These weapons were fired from ships and on land, and did much damage to both people and property. These were not the only weapons used, however. When meeting the enemy in face-to-face battle, swords and sabres were often unsheathed as well.

SWORDS AND SABRES

The swords and sabres used in the War of 1812 were often an indication of the owner's rank. Those carried by high-ranking officers tended to have more embellishment on the hilt and have a more rapier-type blade than those of lower ranks. Sabres were known for their curved blades. However, some swords also had a slight curve. Blade length ranged from 66 to 81 centimetres.

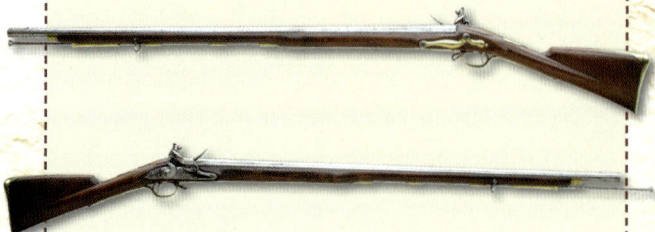

FLINTLOCK MUSKETS

Flintlock muskets were a primary weapon for both the U.S. and British forces. Using these weapons allowed soldiers to fire three or four shots in a minute. The muskets were loaded with paper cartridges that contained both the gunpowder charge and the ball. A piece of flint struck the hardened steel hammer, creating a spark that ignited the gunpowder. Soldiers' cartridge-boxes contained 30 to 60 pre-wrapped cartridges with a measured amount of powder and a lead ball. When commanded to load, soldiers bit off the tip of the paper cartridge and poured a small amount of powder into the powder pan. The remainder of the powder, along with the ball and paper wrapping, were rammed down the barrel using a metal rod that was carried under the musket's barrel. When commanded to fire, soldiers squeezed the trigger, causing the flint in the hammer to drop and strike the powder in the pan. The resulting flash ignited the powder inside the barrel. When firing in volleys, large clouds of smoke were released, thereby reducing visibility on the field of battle.

RIFLES

Even though they were similar in appearance, rifles and muskets were different weapons. Rifle barrels were manufactured with a series of spiraling grooves called rifling. These grooves sent the ball spinning when it fired. The spin made the rifle much more accurate than the musket. However, soldiers found that the rifle was much slower to load than a musket, and in the heat of battle, gunpowder residue made it difficult to load. As a result, muskets were used by the vast majority of soldiers.

CANNONS

Several types of cannons were used in the War of 1812. These included ship cannons and moveable cannons that were mounted on wooden wheels and pulled by horses. Cannons were described by the poundage of the iron cannon balls they fired. Thus, cannons were referred to as six-pounders, twelve-pounders, and so on. Cannons could fire a variety of solids to achieve different effects. Grapeshots, for instance, were made up of loosely packed metal pieces that resembled grape clusters. When shot from the cannon, the pieces spread out to cause damage to a wider area.

MORTARS

Mortars had shorter barrels than cannons and were usually placed in a wooden box at a 45-degree angle. Mortars fired hollow **projectiles** called "bombs" that were filled with gunpowder. Immediately before firing, a fuse was placed in a hole in the bomb. The length of the fuse was based on when the soldiers wanted the bomb to explode. The flame created by firing the mortar lit the fuse. When the fuse burned into the bomb, the powder inside exploded, sending large fragments of the bomb out in various directions. This explosive capability made the mortar a popular weapon for firing at lines of soldiers. Because the mortar's elevation could not be adjusted, the gunpowder charge was varied for the desired range.

HOWITZERS

Howitzers resembled the mortar, except that their elevation could be adjusted. As a result, the howitzer could be fired in an arc like a mortar or in a flat trajectory like a cannon. Howitzers were often placed on wooden carriages for ease of movement on the battlefield.

Important Battles

The U.S. was confident when entering the war. Great Britain was busy fighting France. It seemed that, without strong British support, the Canadian colonies would quickly succumb to U.S. forces. It soon became apparent, however, that the U.S. had misjudged the capabilities of the British and Canadians. The war lasted almost three years. During that time, Canadian and British soldiers, along with their Aboriginal allies, proved they could hold their own.

Battle of Detroit, 1812

In the days leading up to the War of 1812, the United States began taking steps to secure what it considered its strongholds along the border. One of these key positions was Fort Detroit, which was directly across from the Upper Canadian town of Sandwich, present-day Windsor, Ontario. William Hull, the governor of Michigan, recommended that the military presence at Fort Detroit be increased so that he could do battle with both the British and the Aboriginals who were siding with the British. The U.S. government agreed with the recommendations and made Hull the commander of the reinforced army. Shortly after war was declared, Hull led his troops over to Sandwich, where he demanded that the Canadians surrender. When the surrender did not happen as quickly as he had hoped, Hull retreated back to Detroit.

▌ Tecumseh first met Isaac Brock on August 14, 1812. The two men bonded quickly and were able to plan effective battle strategies together.

▌ About a week before the Battle of Detroit, a militia force put together by General Hull experienced defeat at the Battle of Brownstown. This battle led Hull to believe that he was outnumbered by the British and Aboriginal soldiers in the area.

Still, Hull's actions had attracted the attention of British leaders. Sensing a possible threat, Major General Isaac Brock headed to the area with a small army of regulars and militia. When he reached Amherstburg, on the Detroit River, he was joined by Shawnee chief Tecumseh and his warriors. As Tecumseh's warriors harassed the U.S. soldiers and cut off their communications, Brock used the British navy's control of Lake Erie to capture several American ships. Among the papers in one of these ships were Hull's plans. Brock learned from these papers that the Americans' morale was low.

On this basis, Brock decided an immediate attack was best. On August 15, Brock began firing cannons at the fort from the Canadian side of the river. The next day, Brock and Tecumseh crossed the Detroit River and laid siege to Hull's forces at Fort Detroit. Brock dressed 400 militia in British regulars' clothes to disguise his soldier's lack of training. Knowing that Hull and many Americans were frightened of his Aboriginal allies, Brock warned Hull that if he did not surrender immediately, the British commander might not be able to restrain them. He then began bombarding the fort with the few cannons at his disposal. Hull, whose forces outnumbered the British by nearly 2 to 1, put up little resistance to the British attack and surrendered to the British before the day's end.

Hull surrendered Fort Detroit without consulting with his senior officers. As a result, he was arrested and put on trial. While he was initially sentenced to execution, he was later granted a pardon and was allowed to retire from the military.

Battle of Queenston Heights, 1812

Following his victory at Detroit, Brock raced back to the Niagara region to prepare for a possible invasion across the Niagara River. Here, he scattered his few troops along the entire length of the Niagara frontier. The bulk of his forces were stationed at Fort Erie and Chippawa, where he expected the U.S. might attack. Brock wished to initiate an attack on the U.S., but an **armistice** prevented this and gave the U.S. soldiers free rein of the river.

In the early morning hours of October 13, U.S. General Stephen Van Rensselaer and 3,000 soldiers set out across the narrowest part of the Niagara River toward the small village of Queenston to begin the second prong of the U.S. invasion. Van Rensselaer lacked military experience, and several of his officers disagreed with the battle plan.

In the silence of the morning, the sound of oars carried across the Niagara River and alerted the British troops, who began firing. Under heavy fire from the 300 British troops, the first wave of Americans landed below the village. Although the British soldiers prevented Van Rensselaer from capturing the town, the Americans discovered a hidden path to the top of the Niagara **escarpment**. They were able to seize the cannon that had been firing at their reinforcements and gain control of the battle.

▌ Van Rensselaer was born into a wealthy family and, at the time of the war, was heir to one of New York's largest estates.

▌ By the afternoon of the battle, British troops were fighting a U.S. force that was more than 1,000 strong.

Awakened by the sound of **artillery**, Brock quickly mounted his horse and rode from Fort George to the battle. There, he sent a message to Fort George, ordering more troops. However, not wanting to wait, Brock stormed the escarpment without the reinforcements. Half-way up the heights, Brock was struck in the chest with a musket ball. He died instantly.

The reinforcements arrived at the battle later that day and began firing on the U.S. forces, which were still crossing the river. It was only a matter of time before the Americans were defeated. This victory, following shortly after Brock's capture of Detroit, raised the Upper Canadians' morale and convinced them that they could resist their larger neighbour to the south.

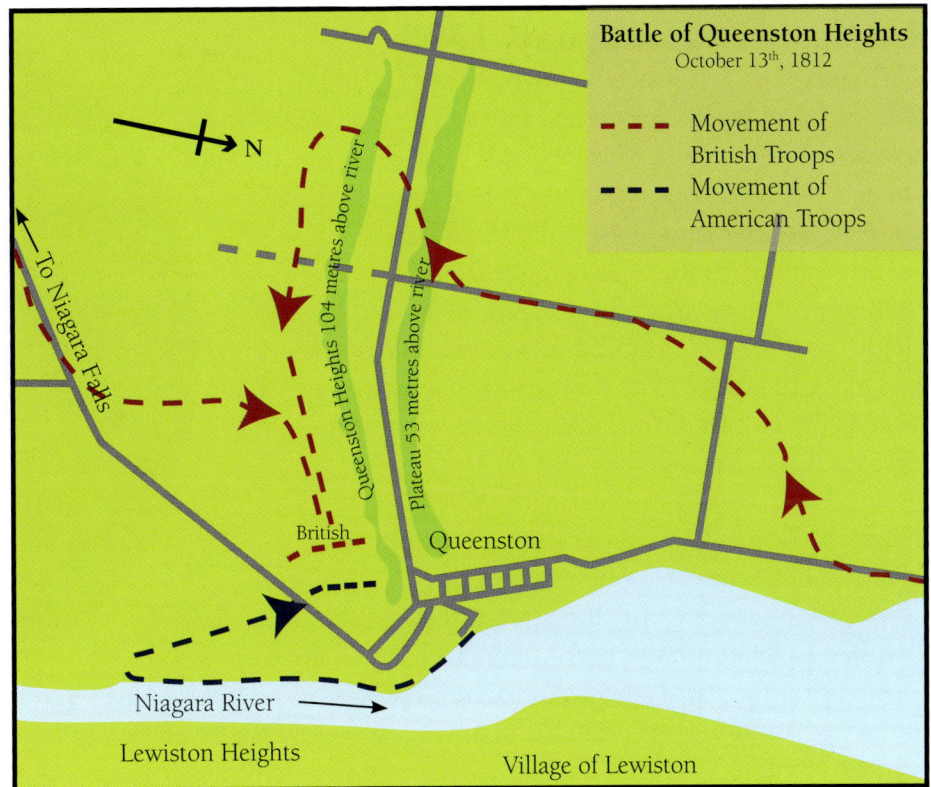

Battle of Queenston Heights
October 13th, 1812

- - - Movement of British Troops
- - - Movement of American Troops

N

To Niagara Falls

Queenston Heights 104 metres above river

Plateau 53 metres above river

British

Queenston

Niagara River →

Lewiston Heights

Village of Lewiston

▌ Brock led the attack up the escarpment. In his red and gold jacket, he was an easy target for U.S. sharpshooters.

"Crowds of the United States Militia remained on the American bank of the river, to which they had not been marched in any order, but run as a mob; not one of them would cross. They had seen the wounded re-crossing; they had seen the Indians, and were panic-struck."

- D. Thompson, History of the Late War between Great Britain and the United States, Niagara, 1832.

Battle of Châteauguay, 1813

By August, 1813, it was obvious that the U.S. plan of capturing Upper Canada had failed. The U.S. forces now sought to capture Montréal and isolate Upper Canada. The plan was twofold. One group of U.S. soldiers, led by Major General James Wilkinson, would head down the St. Lawrence from Sackets Harbor, on Lake Ontario. The other group, led by Major General Wade Hampton, would come north via Lake Champlain. The two groups planned to meet at the mouth of the Châteauguay River and proceed to Montreal.

When the British learned of General Hampton's advance, Lieutenant Colonel Charles de Salaberry hastened his troops to the Châteauguay River. On October 21, Hampton crossed the border with a force of about 3,000 men and advanced up the Châteauguay toward Montreal. Anticipating where the enemy would cross the river, de Salaberry ordered his men to erect a barricade of felled trees placed so that their sharpened ends faced the enemy. He stationed his men strategically around the barricade.

■ Wilkinson had trained to become a doctor before entering military service during the American Revolutionary War.

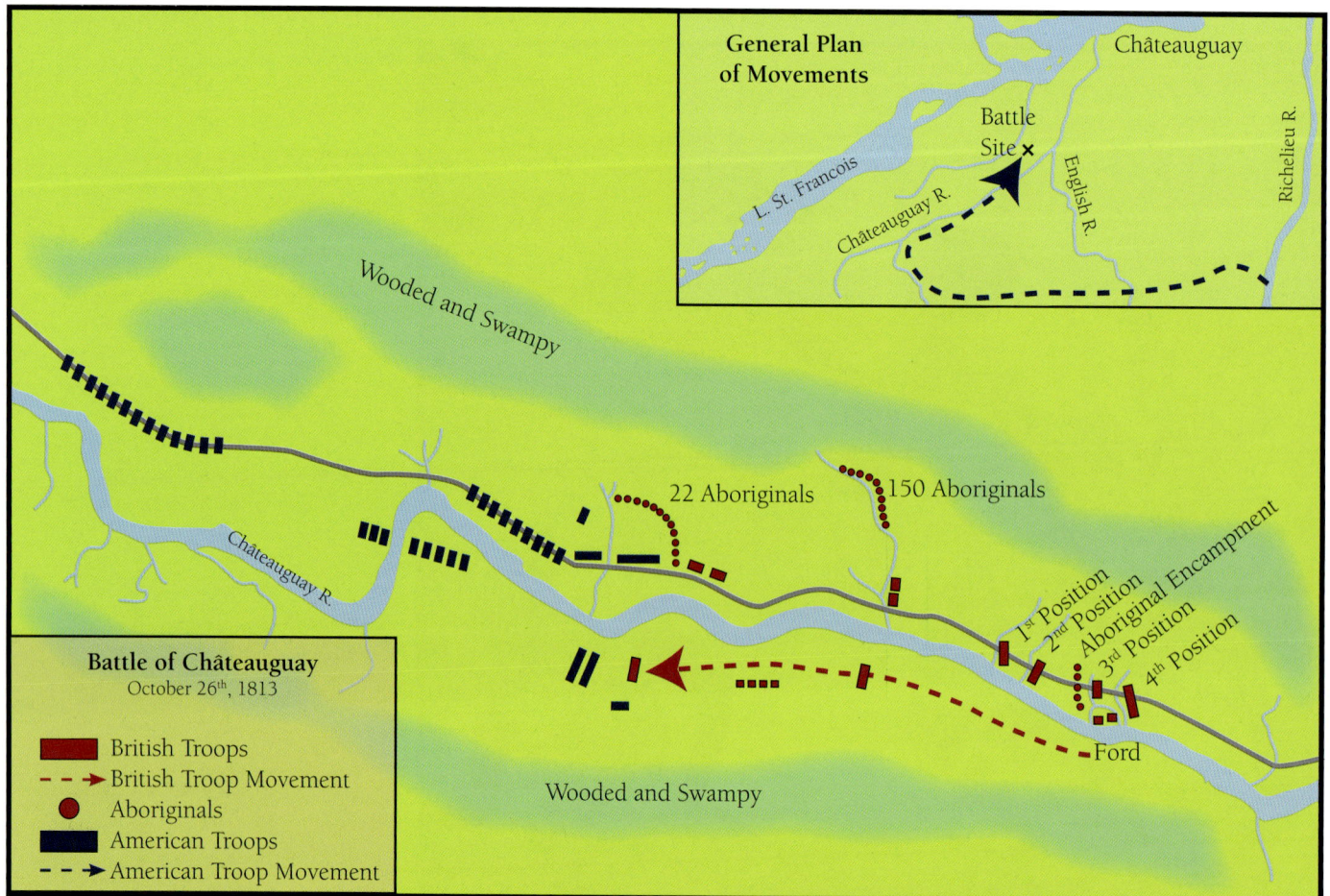

General Plan of Movements

Châteauguay

Battle Site ✗

L. St. Francois

Châteauguay R.

English R.

Richelieu R.

Battle of Châteauguay
October 26th, 1813

■ British Troops
- - -▶ British Troop Movement
● Aboriginals
■ American Troops
- - -▶ American Troop Movement

Wooded and Swampy

Châteauguay R.

22 Aboriginals

150 Aboriginals

1st Position
2nd Position
Aboriginal Encampment
3rd Position
4th Position

Ford

Wooded and Swampy

The Voltigeurs played a key role in the Battle of Châteauguay.

Since the U.S. forces greatly outnumbered the Canadians, de Salaberry ordered his men to make a great deal of noise and to march in a circle. This would give the appearance that reinforcements were pouring into the camp. After about four hours of fighting on October 26, Hampton ordered his troops to retreat. About 1,700 Canadians had defeated 3,000 Americans. After hearing about Hampton's withdrawal, Wilkinson decided not to attack Montreal, and the city was not seriously threatened for the remainder of the war.

Charles de Salaberry came from a family with strong military roots. The family's military service stretched back generations, from service in the French Army to service in the North American colonies.

The Home Front

Unlike Canada's more recent wars, the home front in the War of 1812 was always close to the conflict. The war took place in people's homes and on their land. Fear of invasion and death was a constant for settlers in the battle areas. Still, they had to continue living their lives the best they could. Houses were built, land was farmed, and the colonies were governed even as the cannon balls flew.

Government in British North America

In 1812, each colony in British North America had a similar form of government. At the head of Lower Canada was a governor, while Upper Canada was led by a lieutenant-governor. These positions were appointed, and the appointees could be removed only by the British government. These officials had more power in the colony than the monarch had in Great Britain. Bills could not become laws until the officials signed them. Great Britain could, however, veto or reject any law passed by the colony within two years.

The Executive and Legislative Councils were the most important political bodies in British North America. The Legislative Council drew up laws that the governor or lieutenant-governor could pass. The Executive Council advised the governor or lieutenant-governor and carried out the laws. The governor or lieutenant-governor appointed the members of both councils. The two councils worked closely together, and some people sat on both councils. Most councillors were chosen from among the wealthy, well-educated citizens of the colony.

The Assembly was the least important political body in the colonies. Each colony was divided into voting districts that elected representatives to its Assembly. The Assembly raised money through taxes and drew up bills for the colony. These bills did not become laws until they were approved by the Legislative Council and signed by the governor or lieutenant-governor.

■ Upper Canada's first legislature met in 1792.

■ Fort York is now a National Historic Site in the city of Toronto.

The colonial governments were not immune to U.S. attack. The Assembly building of Upper Canada became one of the war's casualties. When U.S. forces attacked York, Upper Canada's capital city, in April 1813, they burned the building down.

▮ Settlers normally built all of the buildings on their property in the same style using the same materials.

A Settler's Home

When arriving in the Canadas, a settler's first job was to build a home. The first home was often a quickly built log cabin, with only one or two rooms. These houses were seldom more than 4 metres high. They had earth floors, no cellars, and roofs made of bark or hollowed logs. Windows were covered with oiled paper rather than glass. The spaces between the rounded logs were filled with moss, mud, or wood chips. A large fireplace served as a stove and furnace, and was sometimes the only source of light.

As soon as they could, the settlers would build bigger and better homes. The style of these houses depended upon the settler's taste and income, as well as the building materials available. Scottish settlers at Kingston, Ontario, used nearby quarries to build stone homes. Many English immigrants preferred brick buildings. Loyalists often built with timber.

It was in one of these timber houses that Laura Secord's story began. The family had been forced to **billet** U.S. soldiers in its home. One evening, she heard the soldiers discussing their plans to launch an attack on Beaver Dams. She began her courageous journey to find Lieutenant FitzGibbon shortly after.

▮ Laura Secord's home has been restored and is now a popular tourist destination in southern Ontario.

Working the Land

The farther settlers were from town, the more dependent each family was upon its own resources. Traversing the land was difficult, so settlers had to do almost everything themselves, from making their own clothes to growing their own food. Crops grown included oats, wheat, barley, flax, peas, turnips, and hay.

Most farm work was done by hand. While wealthier immigrants to Canada could buy land that was already cleared and producing crops, poorer settlers had to clear the land themselves. The settlers cut down and removed the trees, gradually cleared the stumps and rocks, ploughed the fields, and planted crops. Farmers planted seeds by hand and harvested the grain with **scythes**. They gathered the grain with wooden rakes.

The wood cut during clearing did not go to waste. It was used to construct houses and other buildings and as fuel.

Much effort went into clearing the land and planting and harvesting the crops. During the war, these efforts were sometimes destroyed by battles on farmers' fields. Such was the case in November 1813, when British and U.S. soldiers met in the wheat fields of John Crysler's farm. The battle only lasted a few hours, but by the time it ended, the bodies of U.S. soldiers were strewn across the field, on top of Crysler's fall wheat crop.

Courtship and Marriage

Even with the colonies at war, men and women still found time to marry. Due to the number of soldiers in the area, men far outnumbered women. Soldiers had to obtain permission to marry from their commanding officer. Women had to have the permission of their parents.

The parents considered the man's age, his religion, his political beliefs, and whether the daughter was needed at home. Above all, the man had to be able to support a wife and family.

Once a couple was engaged, the man made frequent visits to her home, and the couple attended church regularly. Among Canada's early settlers, the average age of marriage for women was just under 21 years. For men, it was almost 26 years. Weddings were generally small, with only the families and close friends invited.

Courting took place at balls, skating and sleighing parties, picnics, or church activities.

A Soldier's Life

The soldiers of the War of 1812 lived an unhealthy life. They were exposed to inclement weather, poor food, and inadequate rest.

Most soldiers were housed in barracks or blockhouses. Made from logs, these buildings had slots to allow the soldiers to fire against attackers who had penetrated the main defences. However, the slots also let the air in. This made the barracks drafty and difficult to heat. As the number of soldiers increased, the army rented accommodations in barns, or erected huts and tents.

In the field, the standard daily **ration** consisted of 450 grams of flour, 450 grams of fresh beef or 250 grams of pork, 40 grams of pork or 85 grams of butter, 200 millilitres of peas, and 32 grams of rice. In addition to the monotony of this diet, its caloric intake was inadequate for men doing strenuous work.

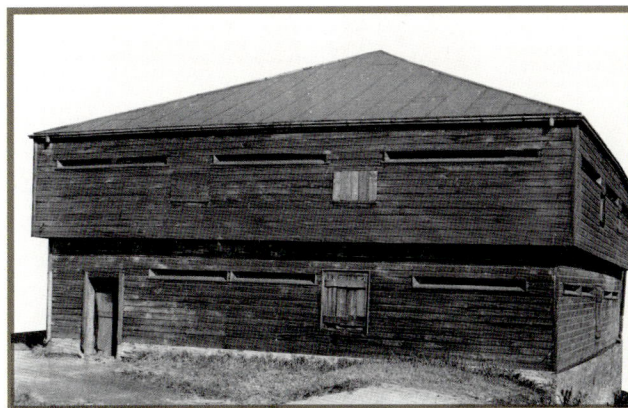

▌ Blockhouses at Fort York featured the loophole slots through which riflemen fired their guns.

A low-ranking regular soldier received one shilling per day and was provided with new clothing to replace worn-out uniforms. A soldier in the militia received much the same pay and rations as his regular counterparts. Most often he was a farmer with no military experience or training.

▌ Soldiers carried few items with them. Bowls filled with brick dust were used to clean their muskets. Lap desks helped hold paper when writing reports. Canvas bags held the small items soldiers needed on a daily basis.

The War Comes to an End

By 1814, Great Britain had been at war with Napoleon for 11 years. The British public demanded peace. Negotiations in the European town of Ghent took the greater part of a year. No mention was made of the problems that had originally caused friction between the two nations, and the matter of British sailors searching U.S. vessels was ignored.

In terms of men, money, and materials, the cost of this tragic struggle cannot be calculated with any degree of accuracy. Unreliable official reports suggest British losses were 5,300 killed, wounded, or missing, while the U.S. suffered a total of about 6,800 casualties. Deaths from disease among the regulars, militia, and Aboriginal Peoples would add substantially to the totals.

▌ Ghent is located in Belgium. However, in 1812, its ownership was being disputed between France and the United Kingdom of the Netherlands.

▌ A plaque is fixed to the building where the U.S. negotiators stayed during the treaty meetings in Ghent.

The **Treaty** of Ghent was signed on December 24, 1814. Under the terms of the treaty, the boundaries of North America reverted to where they had been before the war. Three years later, the Rush-Bagot Agreement limited the number of armed vessels each country could have on the Great Lakes. In 1818, the Anglo-American Convention set the boundary line between the Lake of the Woods and the Rockies at the 49th parallel, thus forming the boundary between Canada and the United States that exists to this day. Except for a provision that prohibited U.S. citizens from fishing in the waters off the Maritime colonies, the treaty left no aggrieved nation or reason to renew hostilities.

▍ Even though the treaty was signed in December, fighting did not stop until February of the following year. This was how long it took for communication to reach all battlegrounds.

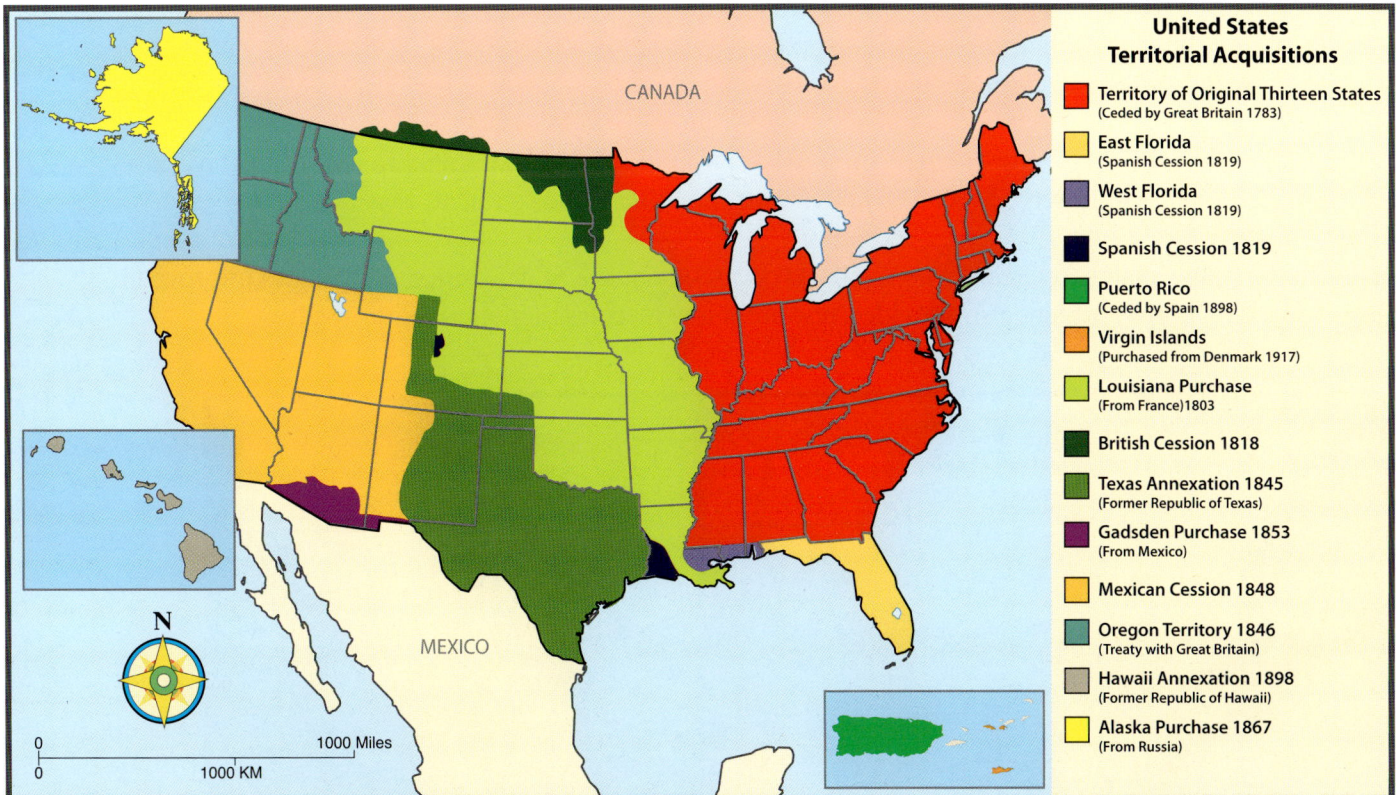

United States Territorial Acquisitions

- Territory of Original Thirteen States (Ceded by Great Britain 1783)
- East Florida (Spanish Cession 1819)
- West Florida (Spanish Cession 1819)
- Spanish Cession 1819
- Puerto Rico (Ceded by Spain 1898)
- Virgin Islands (Purchased from Denmark 1917)
- Louisiana Purchase (From France)1803
- British Cession 1818
- Texas Annexation 1845 (Former Republic of Texas)
- Gadsden Purchase 1853 (From Mexico)
- Mexican Cession 1848
- Oregon Territory 1846 (Treaty with Great Britain)
- Hawaii Annexation 1898 (Former Republic of Hawaii)
- Alaska Purchase 1867 (From Russia)

CANADA

MEXICO

N

0   1000 Miles
0   1000 KM

▍ The boundaries set as a result of the Anglo-American Convention were just one step in the creation of the United States as it is known today.

War cannot be completely resolved on a piece of paper. There are always residual issues and conditions that affect the peoples of the countries involved. The War of 1812 was no different. While the War of 1812 brought some positive changes to British North America, it also created new problems and, in some cases, failed to bring resolution to pre-existing issues.

Impact on Aboriginal Peoples

The only people who truly lost in the War of 1812 were the Aboriginal Peoples south and west of the Great Lakes. Several Aboriginal chiefs complained that Great Britain had not consulted them during the treaty process and that the U.S. showed no respect toward them at all. In fact, the U.S. had begun implementing a removal policy that required Aboriginals east of the Mississippi River to move west of the river. Many Aboriginals moved north to the Canadas as a result.

▮ Many Aboriginal People adopted European clothing as European culture steadily gained influence in North America.

In the north, the Upper Canadian government sought to assimilate the First Nations. It began encouraging First Nations to move onto reserves, learn farming skills, and become Christians. Soon, the traditional lands of the First Nations were open to general settlement.

Construction

During the war, Great Britain spent lavishly on fortifications in Halifax. It soon became the strongest fortress outside Europe and the major base for trade with the British West Indies. When the war ended, Great Britain rebuilt the forts at York and Kingston, and continued to build up its fortifications. Most of the construction projects occurred along the St. Lawrence River.

One of Great Britain's main construction projects was to build the Rideau Canal to link Kingston and Ottawa. The canal would serve as an alternative wartime water route to the St. Lawrence.

The United States matched Great Britain's efforts on its side of the St. Lawrence, working to improve its forts as well. The government also provided resources for the construction of better roads.

▮ The construction of the Rideau Canal was supervised by Lieutenant-Colonel John By of the Royal Engineers.

Nationalism

If anyone could claim victory in the War of 1812, it was Canada. Ten American armies crossed into Canada, but all were driven out. As a result, the Canadas experienced a growth of **nationalism**. Although British troops did most of the fighting, a myth emerged that the settlers had borne the brunt of the fighting.

In Lower Canada, French and English Canadians had put aside their political and economic disagreements to defend their country. The war confirmed the people's ties to Great Britain and their distrust of the United States. The new political leaders in Upper Canada used service in the war as a yardstick to judge a person's loyalty.

Anti-Americanism spread throughout the land. It was most evident in legislation that branded every U.S. immigrant who had settled in Upper Canada after 1783 as an "alien." These people were not allowed to vote, buy government land, or hold public office.

"Madison and his faction of British haters and war adventurers naturally supposed, that...our country would fall an easy prey to his ambition; Great Britain would be humbled at the feet of Napoleon, and France and the United States would then divide the power and commerce of Europe and America. But British and Canadian loyalty, patriotism, and courage defeated their dark designs against the liberties of mankind.

- E. Ryerson: the Loyalists of America and Their Times, Toronto, 1880.

Economy

The war brought lasting economic benefits to British North America. Large sums of British money spent on food and war supplies brought a degree of prosperity previously unknown. Many Maritime vessels engaged in **privateering** during the war and captured more than 200 American ships. These ships and their cargoes were auctioned for huge profits. In Newfoundland, the island's residents gained control of the fishery. Previously, fishing fleets from England had prevented Newfoundlanders from fishing in the Grand Banks. Now, these British vessels and their men were needed for the navy.

As a result of the Napoleonic Wars, Great Britain turned to British North America for the fir, oak, and pine needed to construct warships. New Brunswick and the Ottawa River Valley, in particular, soon rang with the sound of axes as lumbermen felled, hauled, and rafted squared timber to coastal towns for shipment to Great Britain. Soon, a flourishing shipbuilding industry would also emerge.

▐ People made rafts out of the lumber they wanted to sell. They then navigated them down the river to the nearest city. Upon arrival, they dismantled the raft and sold the lumber.

By The Numbers

British and U.S. Troops

When the War of 1812 began, the British army had about 4,500 men and the U.S. had about 7,000. By the time the war ended, each side had more than quadrupled its troop count.

Source: Burnham, Robert. The British Army in the Napoleonic Wars: Manpower Stretched to the Limits?

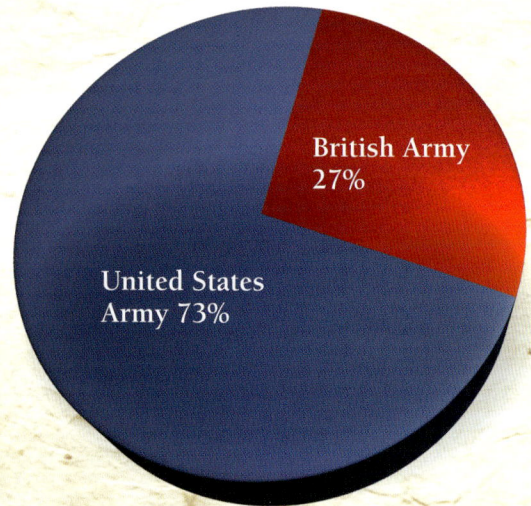

British Army 27%

United States Army 73%

Soldiers by Region

British soldiers served in three main divisions. These were the infantry, the artillery, and the cavalry. Most of the troops were stationed in the Canadas, but there was a contingent in the Maritimes that guarded British interests there.

Regiments	Canadas	Maritimes
Infantry	40	13
Artillery	15	8
Cavalry	1	0

Source: www.warof1812.ca

= 1 Infantry Battalions

= 1 Artillery Companies

= 1 Calvary Regiment

0   400 Kilometres

Source: www.warof1812.ca

N

Occupations of the British Regular Army

British soldiers came from all walks of life. This chart shows the occupational backgrounds of the soldiers. Many of these occupations were useful to the army during the war.

Casualties of War

The U.S. had more than 6,500 casualties during the War of 1812. The British had about 5,300. These numbers include only soldiers who were killed or wounded as a result of fighting. Many other soldiers lost their lives during the war. They died as a result of disease and illness caused by the conditions they lived in.

Wounded 67%

Killed 33%

American Troops

Wounded 70%

British Troops

Killed 30%

Percentage of Occupations in the British Regular Army

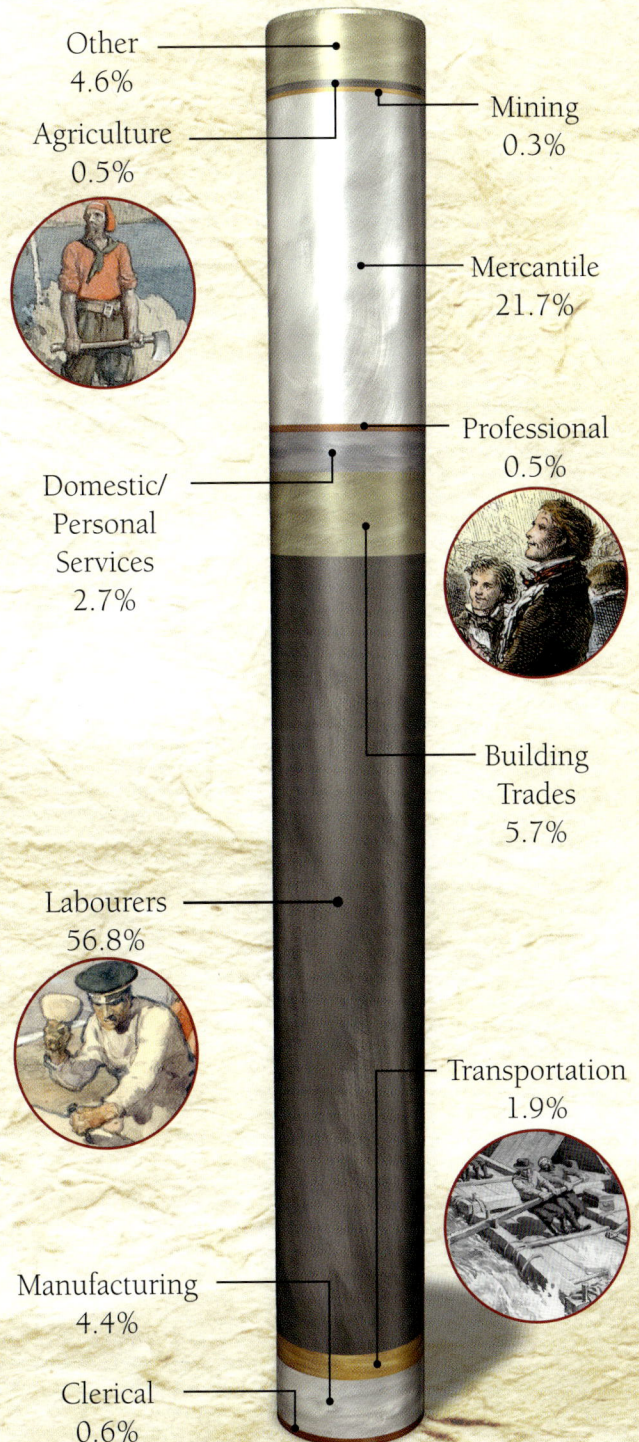

Other
4.6%

Agriculture
0.5%

Mining
0.3%

Mercantile
21.7%

Domestic/
Personal
Services
2.7%

Professional
0.5%

Building
Trades
5.7%

Labourers
56.8%

Transportation
1.9%

Manufacturing
4.4%

Clerical
0.6%

Due to rounding, percentages may not total to 100%.

Theatres of War

In Canada, much emphasis is placed on the War of 1812 battles that took place in British North America. It is important, however, to remember that the War of 1812 was fought in other parts of North America as well. The War of 1812 had three main theatres, or battle areas. The Canadian theatre was located in and around the Great Lakes. The Chesapeake theatre stretched along the east coast of the United States. The New Orleans theatre was situated in and around the Gulf of Mexico. In all theatres, the battles took place both on land and on water.

Chesapeake Theatre

The British used their naval supremacy to blockade the entire east coast of the United States. The area covered by the blockade was small initially, including just the area around Chesapeake Bay and the Delaware River. These waters were important because they provided access to the U.S. capital. However, as the war progressed, the British saw reason to extend the blockade even farther. By 1814, it extended all the way from Maine to South Carolina.

Baltimore
Godly Wood
Bladensburg
Washington
Alexandria
Benedict
Hampton
DELWARE
MARYLAND
British Naval Blockade

LEGEND

→ British Movements

······▶ British Naval Blockade

→ American Movements

☆ Battle Sites

⚑ Fort

● City

New Orleans Theatre

The fight for the southern United States came late in the war. This was mainly because the area was still primarily held by Spain. Only New Orleans and its surroundings were firmly U.S. property. For most of the war, the British did not feel that attacking it was a priority. This changed in 1814, when the war in Europe came to an end. The British were able to free ships for use in an attack on the Americans' southern holdings. The ships did not reach the area until after the Treaty of Ghent had been signed. Due to the poor communication of the time, the British did not know that the War of 1812 had come to an end. They attacked the U.S. forces in New Orleans and suffered a humiliating defeat.

Canadian Theatre

The United States saw several advantages to invading the British colonies to the north. They could use the land for expansion and remove the strong British influence from the area. The United States thought it would have support from the Loyalists and the British and French Canadian colonists. Instead, the residents of Upper Canada sided with the British, making a successful invasion impossible.

How We Remember

The War of 1812 was a pivotal event in Canadian history. Its primary impact on British North America was the increase in national pride. No longer were people just settlers in a new land. They now shared the common bond of experiencing an event together. Heroes were created from this war, and a history began to take shape.

Brock's Monument

Following his death, Isaac Brock was temporarily interred in the northeast bastion of Fort George. Twelve years later, a 30-metre stone monument was erected in his honour on the heights near the spot where he died. His remains were reburied beneath the monument. In 1840, the monument was damaged by a blast of gunpowder. It was rebuilt in 1856. Today, Brock's Monument overlooks the longest undefended border in the world. The monument is a focal point of the Queenston Heights National Historic Site.

Battle of Châteauguay National Historic Site

The site where the Battle of Châteauguay took place has been designated a National Historic Site by the Canadian government. Visitors can walk the grounds and tour the interpretive centre, which explains the events leading up to the battle and the battle itself. A monument on the grounds commemorates the battle. It was erected in 1895 on behalf of the Canadian parliament.

Crysler's Farm Battlefield National Historic Site

The land on which Crysler's farm once sat was flooded during the construction of the St. Lawrence Seaway. However, a monument now sits on nearby Crysler Park. The monument is made of granite and has a cannon on each side. A building close to the monument houses artifacts from the time and provides an audio-visual presentation on the battle.

Memorials and other symbols of remembrance began to appear in areas where battles took place. As the country grew, the sites where many of the events took place took on added importance. Several were granted official historic site status by the government and were restored to their former state.

Laura Secord Monument

A monument dedicated to the courageous actions of Laura Secord can be found on the Queenston Heights overlooking the Niagara River. The monument comprises a column with an oval plaque in the centre. The plaque has Secord's likeness engraved on it.

Valiants Memorial

In 2006, the Valiants Memorial was unveiled in Ottawa. The memorial features statues of 14 people who are considered key figures in Canada's military history. Three of these statues feature the likenesses of people from the War of 1812. Sir Isaac Brock, Charles de Salaberry, and Laura Secord are all memorialized for the roles they played in Canadian history.

Fort York National Historic Site

The Fort York National Historic Site is situated where the Battle of York took place in 1813. Fort York is known as the birthplace of what later became the city of Toronto. The site features the largest collection of original War of 1812 buildings in Canada. The fort offers tours and stages re-creations of military life in the 1800s.

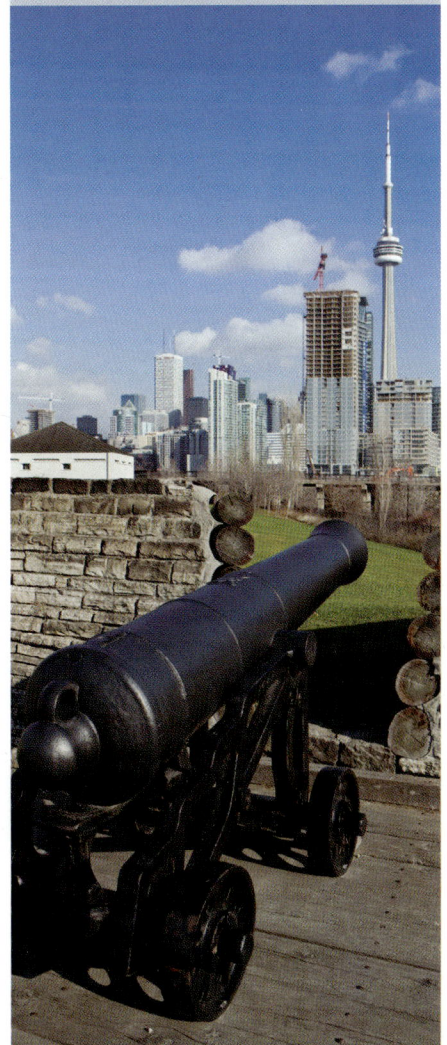

Timeline

The Battlefield

June 18, 1812 President James Madison of the United States declares war on Great Britain.

October 13, 1812 Isaac Brock is killed during the Battle of Queenston Heights.

July 17, 1812 The U.S. surrenders Fort Michilimackinac to Major-General Isaac Brock.

August 15 to 16, 1812 The Battle of Detroit takes place.

1812

The Home Front

June 21, 1813 Laura Secord overhears U.S. soldiers discussing a plot to attack the British at Beaver Dams.

June 22, 1813 Laura Secord begins a two-day journey to Beaver Dams to warn the British of the impending attack.

June 24, 1813
Thanks to Laura Secord's actions, the British win the Battle of Beaver Dams.

October 26, 1813
Charles de Salaberry is victorious over U.S. forces at the Battle of Châteauguay.

April 27, 1813
U.S. forces attack Fort York and burn the settlement down.

November 11, 1813
British forces successfully defend their land at the Battle of Crysler's Farm.

December 24, 1814
The Treaty of Ghent is signed, ending the War of 1812.

April 27, 1813
The Assembly building of Upper Canada is burned down during the Battle of York.

Test Yourself

Multiple Choice

1. Which US President declared war on Great Britain in 1812?
   a. Thomas Jefferson
   b. Andrew Jackson
   c. James Madison
   d. Barack Obama

2. What motivated the U.S. to go to war with Great Britain?
   a. Great Britain's support of Aboriginal Peoples
   b. Maritime rights
   c. War Hawks
   d. All of the above

3. How many people lived in British North America in 1812?
   a. 200,000
   b. 500,000
   c. 1 million
   d. 5 million

4. At what battle was Sir Isaac Brock killed?
   a. Queenston Heights
   b. Detroit
   c. Beaver Dams
   d. Châteauguay

5. What battle did Laura Secord help the British win?
   a. Queenston Heights
   b. Detroit
   c. Beaver Dams
   d. Châteauguay

6. Who led the British forces during the Battle of Châteauguay?
   a. Isaac Brock
   b. James Wilkinson
   c. Charles de Salaberry
   d. Robert Barclay

7. In what town was the peace treaty signed?
   a. Ghent
   b. The Hague
   c. Washington
   d. London

True or False

1. The War of 1812 occurred as a result of the Napoleonic Wars in Europe.

2. Most of the War of 1812 was fought around Lake Ontario.

3. Part of the War of 1812 was fought in the Gulf of Mexico.

4. Laura Secord was born in Massachusetts.

5. The Battle of Châteauguay was a fight for control of Québec City.

6. The Assembly was the most important political body in the colonies.

7. By 1814, Great Britain had been fighting Napoleon for 30 years.

8. Following the war, the government of Upper Canada began moving First Nations onto reserves.

Mix 'n Match

1. Loyalists
2. War Hawks
3. Voltigeurs
4. Tecumseh
5. Shako
6. Flintlock
7. William Hull

a. musket
b. hat
c. settlers from U.S.
d. U.S. politicians
e. Battle of Detroit
f. Shawnee chief
g. Lower Canada militia unit

A Matter of Marching

When the U.S. declared war on Great Britain, it thought the invasion of British North America would be just "a matter of marching" in and taking over. Yet, when the war ended after three years, the U.S. had actually achieved very little. Why was the U.S. not able to succeed in its invasion plans?

Using the Internet, books from the library, and any other resources, research the background to the war and the events that took place that prevented the United States from winning the war.

Be sure to examine the following areas.

• The number of soldiers on each side

• The organization of military forces on each side

• The war strategies and techniques used by each side

• The civilians who participated in the war and their contributions

Make a chart that lists what you found out about each side. Which side appears to have stronger resources? Why?

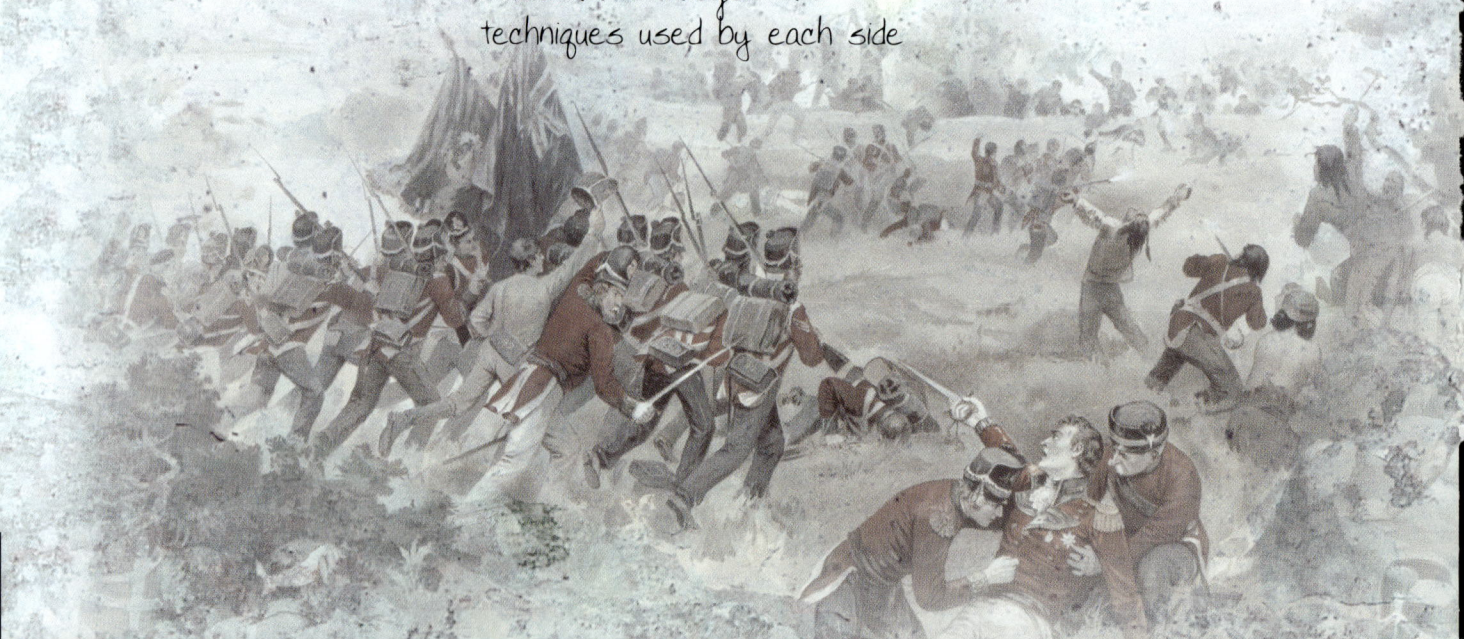

Glossary

American Revolutionary War: the revolution of the U.S. colonies against Great Britain from 1775 to 1783; also called the War of Independence

armistice: a cessation of fighting by mutual consent

artillery: large guns used by an army or the troops that use them

assimilate: to absorb a group of people into the prevailing culture

billet: to provide lodging for troops

blockaded: used ships or military forces to isolate a nation, area, city, or harbour in order to prevent the entrance and exit of traffic and commerce

cartridges: cylindrical casings containing the primer and charge of ammunition for firearms

civilian: a person who is not a member of the military

colony: a territory occupied by a settlement from a ruling state

commission: the rank and authority of an officer in the armed forces

company: a subdivision of a military regiment

deserters: soldiers who have abandoned their post in violation of orders

empire: a grouping of people and land under the rule of a sovereign state

escarpment: a steep slope that separates two relatively level areas of differing elevations

front: the area in which armies face each other

garrison duty: assigned to protect a fortified place

Iroquois Confederacy: a union of several First Nations, including the Mohawk, Oneida, Onondaga, Cayuga, Seneca, and Tuscarora

militia: part-time military

multilateralism: countries working together on an issue

Napoleonic Wars: the wars waged by or against France under Napoleon from 1803 to 1815

nationalism: devotion to the interests of one's own country

privateering: commissioning an armed, privately owned vessel for war service

projectiles: fired, thrown, or otherwise propelled objects

ration: a fixed allowance of specific items, such as food

regiments: military units of ground troops consisting of at least two battalions

regular army: an army made up of professional soldiers

scythes: tools with long handles and long, curved blades that are used for harvesting some crops

sovereignty: complete independence and self-government

treaty: a written agreement between two or more nations

Index